○ + □ ☆

thing is

SUZANNAH SHOWLER

thing is

POEMS

McClelland & Stewart

Library and Archives Canada Cataloguing in Publication

Showler, Suzannah, author
Thing is / Suzannah Showler.

Poems.
Issued in print and electronic formats.
ISBN 978-0-7710-0555-8 (paperback).–ISBN 978-0-7710-0556-5 (epub)

I. Title.

PS8637.H69T45 2017   C811'.6   C2016-904540-4
                                             C2016-904541-2

Published simultaneously in the United States of America by
McClelland & Stewart, a Penguin Random House Company

Library of Congress Control Number is available upon request

ISBN: 978-0-7710-0555-8
ebook ISBN: 978-0-7710-0556-5

Typeset in Minion by M&S, Toronto
Printed and bound in the USA

McClelland & Stewart,
a division of Penguin Random House Canada Limited,
a Penguin Random House Company
www.penguinrandomhouse.ca

1 2 3 4 5   21 20 19 18 17

PERSONAE

O

Concerned with consciousness,
enclosed spaces, negation

+

Concerned with beauty,
sadness, sleep

□

Concerned with haunting,
the afterlife, being a ghost

☆

Concerned with interpersonal
communication, empty spaces, the future

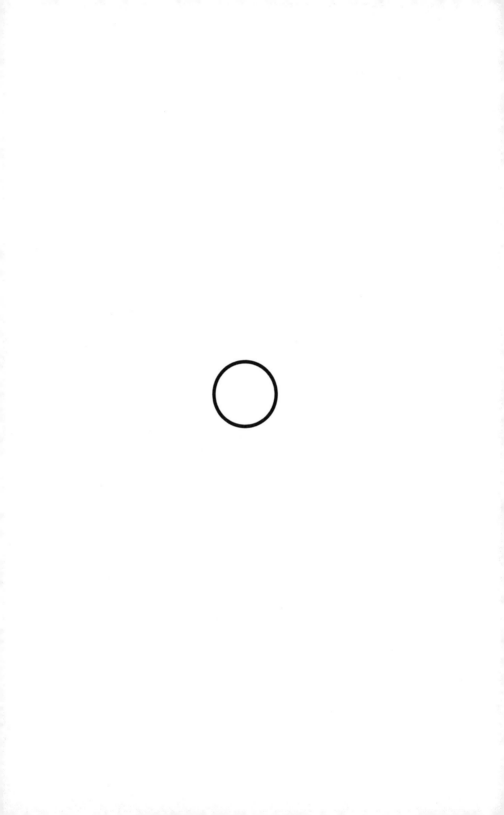

SUBJUNCTIVE MOOD

O

Thoughts: I've been experimenting
with those. Have you heard the one

about the beetle in the box? Kitty
in a box? Thinking never met a box

it didn't want to put a little life
inside. Metal inspired to resist

the elements, or takeout container
closing, cardboard getting real

cozy with more cardboard. See how
recycling can be open and shut.

Reconstitution's in vogue, all
that's solid is old, what we keep

in mind comes back to us. For real,
like, five percent of what we think

is new. The rest is on repeat, each
ribbon slow-writhing like an eel

through a viewfinder, begging to be
clicked and tagged. Have I had

this one before? The new is hard
and brief, like the dumb sparkle

stuck below that woman's eye
while she cries on TV, reaching

for you all the time, the only thing
you see until you don't. Then on to

the next. I want to know where to look
for myself: coming or coming back?

Okay, wait, I've got a good one:
house with infinite rooms, whole

life boxed in each one, no doors,
soundproofing only so-so. Let's say

you're there too. You'll never
know the whole, but you do

hear things, words slipping through,
tracing sounds you think you might

have known before. As though being
is no more than being reminded.

That's all I've got so far. It pretty
much just goes on that way for a while.

CROWD SOURCE

O

Inside the stadium, the screen lights up
the word NOISE, so we all yell at it.
The whole, human afternoon is a maw.
Feel free to swim, go down feeling
a megafauna's heartbeat. It's not
the worst way: right up in it, choosing
together, course-correcting into the dark.

MORNING

O

Light finds formation in lines
on the wall, window copying

itself out as a list of what's lost
when blinds refuse to let a day

into the room whole. Reformed,
stripped down, as if light has big

hopes of being memorized,
cheat sheet of unsettled verbs

in modal forms, ready to pivot
from what is to what will follow.

The blinds are a coping strategy
for the window – that introvert

who deals with the public
all day. Does it seem weird

how light keeps coming up,
showing its face even after

it's been turned away? And
doesn't it have a whole plane

of not-inside to fawn over?
Still it comes around, still

tries to get in. To trace day's
possible outcomes on the wall.

LOOSE CONSCIOUSNESS

O

When asked about my interests,
I've been known to include: being

awake. Which I'm pretty sure
means searching out distraction

from the body's insistence
on function over form. Once

found, I wish it away in favour
of return to rotation in an eddy

of self-contained concerns.
As in, the ones that hold you.

Imagine being the sort to loose
consciousness into a day, like

a dog headbutting a screen door
it doesn't see because it's not

interested in what forms the line
between place and intention.

The repetition makes a sloppy
dent. So now this is physical.

I don't know if we're made
after what we want

or whatever we keep
banging our heads against.

IF I HAD ONE

O

I'd walk my dick like all the neighbours walk
their dogs when they come home from work,
and dark is creeping up the lawn, and supper's
not yet made, but still the dog goes out
because that's the deal we make with pets.
We take them out to pee and smell the air,
and in exchange they keep themselves
from what they want most: to bite some living
thing across the throat until it's dead.
We keep our pets to tame and trick – we call
this love because that's kind of what it is.
My dick would be well loved. I'd socialize
it well. I'd show it all the sights, stroke
its stupid little head, call it what
it likes. You know, I've cared for other people's
dicks before and know just what they want
to hear: *Perfect form! Best in Show!*
You fit exactly where you need to go!
My dick and I would make a handsome pair,
I'm sure. People always say that dicks
and their owners look alike. We'd be a match.
I feel like there are places I might get
to go so long as I have got my dick
on hand, things I've never seen that must be
worth a look. A dick's an outside thing
looking for an in. I'm the other way
around. I wake up feeling things are still
to come, and there's still more to know.
I go to sleep believing I could grow.

YOU'RE NEVER IF YOU'RE NOT

O

Something I've learned by looking
at gaps: all problems can be broken

down into matter, energy, info. Did
you know having organs makes us

rational? Meaning, the parts make
the system. The body is a part

of a project to not not be around
that other thing, keep it in parcel:

rogue eyeball, unthinkable flutter,
less the gear and more the grind.

Maybe. Am I getting closer? Is this
thing on? I have a feeling the gap

won't be filled, but skinned. It's okay,
it's good to have something to look at

while you wait for conditions to make
themselves felt. Do you follow? Will you

get up on my plane? The weather here
is so unbroken. The weather's so flat.

NOT NOT

O

When it comes to classification,
the thing you aren't after isn't

the worst place to start. Pick
one substance, then another,

scan for repeated features.
Look at each instance. Be real:

what is essence, what is
accident? You need to line

up what can be lost. Lists can
be so brutal. Fact: unity comes

in degrees. That said, features
identified through the process

of individuation are not,
in themselves, what make up

the individual. Which is to say,
once you've seen a thing, it isn't

what you're looking for. I used
to know this riddle about what

it is *to be* and *to follow*. It doubled
as a joke about expectations.

The answer was: dog. Joke
was: there was no riddle.

NEVER THE POINT

O

One theory vis-à-vis the origins of language: there is no original language

to speak of, and yet when we speak it makes itself felt, fossilized syntax,

the thing that never was itself but still found in what follows from it –

no dead tongue but ghost tongue, fog-licker, dye drunk up the stem to lay

strata on the bloom, and now we know: there is no surface without a trace.

CONSEQUENCE

O

Wake from the dream of a sequence,
the proposition that *what is* follows

from *what was*. Events don't keep
good tabs on other events. I'm not

saying it hurts to lay down order,
but what you see is only what you get

off on. I mean it's all you. Take this
view: the sky giving up light vague

as the biotic smudge my face leaves
on a phone screen. It's not enough

to predict the future, but it might
put you in your place. Namely, right

up in it. Still, I can't stop turning
over cards, looking for evidence

of what I already know. It always
comes up. So, that's one strategy.

I have others. Like, here's a story
I tell myself: I am right in the middle

of telling a great story. Another
one is, when I think about you,

I google myself. And my mind tells
my other mind: *please use your*

inside voice. Have I told you
my recurring dream yet? Kidding.

That's not my dream – I swiped it.
You know it's true what they say:

when you're a hammer, everything
looks like a less-important hammer.

CONDITIONS

O

Scenario: on the couch, I turn soft. I know
the cover is made from the skin an animal
wore its whole life to mark the difference
between itself and the air. My own borders
are thinning. It's hard to see couch as cow,
but if I'm sinking, it must be my duty
to try. I'm having a hard time with the legs.

Scenario: I'm swallowed by the furniture.
The room keeps turning on an axis only
it can feel. I went willingly, but whole.
Left a note to myself in a code I can't be
bothered to crack. It's right there, the most
ordinary thing. The condition of comfort
doesn't make it any easier to be honest.

Scenario: the couch is a room, and I walk
into it. Everyone knows cows have seven
stomachs, but no one cares what this means
for the grass. I'm going down again and again,
feeling the system in parts. If I could only
have one life, I'd swallow it. And keep coming
back to the same words. I've got you in mind.

NO MATTER

O

Focus on a deviation and the pattern
comes to you – everything original
must repeat. See, here's the morning

looking for recruits, sun poking
its foreshortened finger in your eye.
No matter. Value comes less

through repetition than its absence.
The less you see a thing, the more
you look for it. They say success

is mostly showing up. Or was that
putting on a show? See, I'm pretty
good at parties. I've nailed this one

discourse on what the body doesn't
have going for it. I'm all: *mind
over mind, you know?* This is how

I draw a crowd: lots of scribbled
circles overlapping. Even I can see
this is ordinary. As my own condition,

I'm really feeling myself. Do you see
where this is going? No, I mean it.
I don't know where to get off.

CAN YOU RATE YOUR MOOD?

+

Which I take to mean: does the word
comorbidity feel a little cozy round

the mouth? Some professional advice: snap pics
of your moles beside a ruler every six months.

Progress appeals to me about as much as
reincarnation. That is, enough to delay

the thought a little while longer. Besides,
the best argument for repetition is any

morning, how it's a one-way hinge
on a trapdoor. Then there's the rest:

strangers beetling their way down wet stairs
to the train, umbrellas receding into armpits

like anemones startled by underwater
cameras. The station's creak machine

warning birds: *this is not your resting place.*
Each bird may be a consciousness recycled

to dumb, puttering translucence, who once knew
the cosmos as moving vapours, or took storms

of living things into a basin mouth,
swallowed through the fluttering goodbyes.

Then on to the next. This possibility is one reason
not to kick a pigeon in the chest and watch it try

to flap its way back into gravity's good graces,
even when you know you could. I still recycle,

by the way. Just as I cleave to most civic fictions,
like thumbing the eager button at the crosswalk,

declaring myself to the non-existent registrar
of pedestrians. What if my mind is just

a very long public hearing, and the inevitable
crackpot has been at the mic all the while?

For this, and other reasons, I don't insist
on what I know *comorbidity* should mean:

a kind of love, or brand loyalty. A good excuse
to get the whole gang back together and ruminate.

SOURCE

+

I put a box beside the bed,
and all night long a noise
machine makes the sound
of light. See how loose
consciousness is? Shucks
off at the sound of nothing.
Weird how we've evolved
to let ourselves down so easy.
This is one feature of being
alive: your body needs
to practise dying, like,
thirty percent of the time.
Meanwhile, your mind
has a crack at some new
way to be, whole life boxed
in each night. If you don't
do this, you'll die for real.

ASKING FOR A FRIEND

+

Say you see the same
face each time
you travel the park
that runs the length
of old rail line, same
face on each new body
flickering at you out
of the reclaimed green.
And say the theremin
screams under the
implication of your hand,
turns with you like a mood
ring, stokes a thought
about the origins of language
that repeats. Say you knew
this would happen and still
you touched frequencies,
as though this were any
path to knowledge.
What if you kept pace,
gave up your own vision
to the repeating features
in the day. What if it doesn't
feel like sacrifice. And whatever
moves in the air by mere
nearness turns particular,
as in made of particles,
able to be parted, needing
to be if you want to get
through it. Say it's so
loud you can't
think past. You don't

see a way through
to new anything.
Say your face comes
home with you.

MORNING

+

Wait, what was it about the Knowledge again?
Something about what turns up when scanning

the brains of cabbies who've swallowed whole,
irrational cities in grey matter. The size and shape

of an especially tense child's fist. If I remember right,
the study revealed a lapsed ability to internalize new

linguistic forms. This was just a side note in a story
about how extraordinarily adaptable our structures are,

but of course I'd get stuck circling what goes missing
from the ordinary condition of knowing more than one

should. You know how it is. Now I'm doing my best
imitation of coming back to life after an accident, looking

to the ceiling for new patterns to model all my bright
choices after. Willing influence overhead, as if finding

myself strung closer to plaster spackling on a chain
of causation would be any comfort. All I see is rigging,

the slack organization of thick-braided steel just barely
holding me to the task of staying in another day's worth

of contingencies. Might not sound like it, but the whole
pretense of waking up dead: it's an exercise in gratitude.

A feeling that doesn't come to me so natural. If you can
believe that. Though I have made a habit of weeping

over things not yet lost, as if having them now was only
a shadow cast back by the more tangible absence ahead.

I watch light make its play for control over the wall.
It's still so early. Far be it from me to say what's right.

TURN

+

The alleys wider than the houses they shadow
keep turning up colours charitably described
as muted. Meaning, they aren't talking to you
anymore. It's hard to stop thinking of yourself

as a fuck-up, wondering whether the plot may
turn more interesting with, say, a few sobbing
parties for a chorus. Or more nights you follow,
maybe even join, as they sneak into the new

day's abandoned warehouse. You, too, could
be a part of some crowd of people swimming
through good lighting, looking for themselves
to turn into something new. Have you noticed

how it's always the same, every city patterned
by shadows and colours you forget to look at
after a while? Turns out, you don't ever get too
far from yourself, and once you've seen a thing,

the only real turn-on is remembering when you
hadn't. I know this isn't what you had in mind.
But don't you find there's an unexpected charm?
To feel for a centre and wind up in the middle.

DOWNSTAIRS

+

there lives a thickness
of neighbours, which is

the collective noun
I've coined just now

for these, with their voices
muscling, and their bacon

and pot and banana bread,
who yell shut up shut up

shut up at their dog,
like a finger swiping

to refresh a screen,
cascading new trifles

into a field of view.
At night, I swim through

their bong water,
and the dog stays

too sad and too brown
to love, ugly face studded

with eyes light as tree gunk
hardened over the number

of years we call a period –
whatever happens between

marks left on rocks,
the exchange of heat.

The note that calamity
was here, moved on.

POINT OF ORDER

+

The first matters and then you forget. What follows
is a period of framing yourself across the windows
of parked cars like a row of screengrabs gathered
on your desktop for a future exercise in composites.
Not looking at anything but the fact of being right
up in it, you touch yourself like a new haircut until
it gets old. Somewhere, you misplace the high point.
It's always in the last place you look, and you forget
to go looking. Besides, you're never where you think
you've been. By now, we're mostly down to the count.
The numbers are louder than what punches them out.

HASHTAG NO FILTER

+

The sunset barfs all over
you, says you deserve

the gilding you get,
as if you were built

with a future longing
for this moment in mind.

The light will take back
what it says about you,

and you know it, but still
you stay here now, cash in

on the free, all-access
trial pass to beauty.

Birds gather in perfect
mall-swarm formation,

and clouds grind up
on the horizon, trying

to stoke one last boner
from the sun. Everything

is so crowded with distance.
And you're there, you're right

up in it, thick-covered
with the experience of being

here, dragging the saturation
dial, feeling for the limit.

HASHTAG YOLO

+

Morning is a know-it-all, sending
its bright cast back on night.

Knowing that is enough to keep me
right where I am, haunting these

stairs, recording my slide down
the banister in reverse, on repeat.

The stairs are a well – pit deep
throating wishes in the form

of obsolete coins – and I'm getting
to the bottom of it. Each stair is

a case – the grammar needed to describe
actions imagined but not performed,

or express the wish to not be
quite so *yourself.* For a second.

One night I could love myself,
then ghost. It's only a matter

of time. The stairs are a flight –
a strategy for tasting finer features

in varietals of regret. Pictures
of what was not the case bumping

off what was. Is anything really
an accident? Don't we mean it all

at the time, then times change?
Wanting to take something back

is just hunger for an old intention,
a wish to have it now, then bury it

in your own body. Watch the clip
on repeat, in reverse. A black box

measures change but swallows
every action that causes it.

I hear gravity is a law.
I'll be the spirit and the letter.

OLD WORLD

+

Once, I missed a train and killed
a loose handful of hours idling
in gardens older than the country

I was born in. The light was
a catcall I held off with formal
pronouns, cultivating a distance

I've since folded into regular
rotation in my stock of moods.
This isn't new: stitching a lone

moment to what has followed
from it, as though thinking
through the past is just one

more way to look for yourself.
Still, I feel like telling you how
I drank a bottle of champagne

and peed under the half-barbed
lace of a bush I imagined had been
cultivated to flatter the royal

view. My knowledge of history
always only so-so. Of course I was
approached. When I say I wanted

attention, I mean I was looking
for evidence of being more than
a pronoun set loose in a house

with no rooms, concrete and rebar
sketch of a future that might yet be
forestalled. Even then, I couldn't

not see things in terms of failure.
That I was young and drowning
in light escaped me. From here,

the story is its own shadow,
inhaling the space it's not in.
I'm trying to tell you nothing

happened, but I was still made
after it. I took a different train.
Woke up in a new country.

SINCE YOU ASKED

□

This whole business
about unfinished business
is bullshit. I don't know
where that rumour started,
but it's bad for the new ones,
the way they arrive already
jacked for some mission
to fulfill, as though good
behaviour has rewards,
like anyone's watching.

Thing is, being dead
is just another angle.
Besides, the living look
quite sweet from here,
how they think they move
so mysteriously, how
they're always leaking.

Really, don't get hung
up on the whole death thing.
It's just one gong getting
its begged-for gut punch:
spangled, showy sound, yet
indistinguishable from all
other gongs. Kicks off
the action, but never the point.

That you died will at first
seem special, and you'll want
to tend the moment like a wild,
broken creature you could
nurse back into the world.

That never works. Death loses
mass in its cardboard box,
shedding details until it's too
reduced to even try to bite
the hand you haven't got.
You won't be able
to pinch its windpipe shut,
or bury it in any earth.

What do I like best about being
a ghost? Hard to choose
just one thing. Maybe the soft
wilt of remembering
how you were once alive,
but not *who*. The life lost
becomes featureless, lovely
as sheet metal, directing quick
frames of light into nothing.

SELF-PORTRAIT AS YOGI

☐

I might be the best one
in the class. Never late,
don't make any mess.
You'll never see
my wingspan bust up
someone else's swan dive.

And the heat?
No sweat.

All right. Truth: I do fake
the breathing. But I can find
something else to dilate, feel for
a limit, then slide back to where
it was. I figure air isn't important.
It's the change of scale around it.

I'm not really here to get in shape.
I don't have one of those.

You might be wondering why
I come at all, what with the whole
mind-body link being, here, a bit
unsatisfying to explore.

Here it is: the living pose,
and in between they leave
one thing behind, lean into
the next, waiting to feel a catch.

That's when what follows
living feels, I guess,
like being alive.

We each lean into
our own nothing,
wait for it to push back.

SELF-PORTRAIT AS MISREMEMBERED RIDDLE

☐

I'm not what I am.
If I was what I am,
I wouldn't be what
I am. I'm not what
I follow. If I was, I
wouldn't be what I
am. There wasn't a
thing, then: there it
was. Nothing with
its follow-up. Nice
pic. I'm not what I
say, but I am what
I say I am. I'm not
following. What is
this. If what is and
what is not cannot
be the same thing,
it follows that you
cannot be both the
thing you are plus
the thing you'll be,
which, not yet the
case, has no matter
and therefore isn't.
Like, it just doesn't
work. I'm trying to
say it matters. Say
this is so: how can
I say I intend to do
something? I can't
see what'll be next
and it's already all

laid out anyway. I
am not sure if I am
even here. I don't
know I can't say I
am not I am not I –

SELF-PORTRAIT AS PUNXSUTAWNEY PHIL

□

Outside, the crowd
watches through
their hands,
pushing back
the sun with flat
palms of light.

Evidence is this:
frost tracing marks
on the surface
of what you knew
was there already.

And this is
what the living love,
signs tagging where
what they know begins.

Once, I was a flash
captured at the top
of the stairs.
I moved emulsion,
scattered shards
of silver over plastic
thin as fingernails.

You knew I was
there. Through
the finder, the view.
I showed you
what I could.

But now this is
physical. We all
have something
to prove.

So go ahead, pull me
out of the dark. I'll try
not to bite your hand.

Hold me up
to be captured
by the small
screens, garden
of sequins, swaying
like animals
whose movements
follow from
one to the next,
choosing together.

Ask me if I can see
the space I'm not in.
Whether it looks
like a feeling about
what's coming next.

Lesson learned:
prediction is looking
for yourself.

I don't know
where to look
for myself: coming,
or coming back?

Of course I see
my shadow. Duh,
I'm a ghost.
What's missing
is the other part.

Six more weeks
of anything.

SELF-PORTRAIT AS NOTE TO SELF

☐

Don't come back.

SELF-PORTRAIT IN E-PRIME

□

Assuming it matters which words we use

to describe the status quo, watch me try for

my badge in not talking about what I don't

have going for me. This might feel like

sudden-onset obsolescence, or watching

a photo age-progress in front of you, but all

I've done is stop saying what I couldn't

possibly mean anyway. In this, I exercise

my right to ditch old causes. The living do

it all the time. Though I guess estrangement

doesn't often get staged right in the language

used to describe it happening – I can see

how that might seem fresh. In any case,

from here I only want to look ahead, stay

focused on what keeps coming up. I have

things on my side. Like time, you know?

It protracts like a retired rail line running

its mouth. Or film rolling out, each frame

a willing subject in a research study on do-

overs. All my moments get handed down

to me from elsewhere, come with an image

already printed on one side, though they do seem

game to double-down on exposure. I need that.

I like to picture myself in every landscape

I see. How else to put myself out there,

figuratively speaking? I feel primed to rise

to prominence in a field of view, if you catch

my drift. I kind of lied earlier about not looking

back. In truth, I still have one memory

that's held up surprisingly well given

the current state of affairs. In it, I catch myself

falling down stairs – an event that doesn't

even happen, gets sucked back like thick spit.

Nothing to speak of. Except I had a body

then, and even in its absence now I can't

forget the way it felt to not fall. A whole

system announced itself inside me like a

well-rehearsed chorus I'd never met screaming

a minor note. My skin knew what I didn't:

I had a surface. It registered the change.

SELF-PORTRAIT WITH IPHONE

□

Touch a picture
of a wastebasket
for forgetfulness.
A gear when you
want to change
your fate. This
isn't mechanical,
but if the tooth
fits, there's a bite.
I can drag boxes
from the centre, swipe
to bring on a quick
cascade of the new.
Each moment
arrives like a group
hug, a float in a parade.
My best dick pic
is a panorama,
frames feathered
across the screen.
Nothing to see. No
thing to see here.

HOW TO THINK ABOUT IT

☐

Hard not to think of the afterlife's
umbilical tether to what it isn't
anymore. Time rolls its eyes back
in its head, shows off those filmy
whites. If you could be
what you follow, you wouldn't
be what you are. All right, let's
get into categories. Things being
a has-been is not unlike: vacation
at high altitude, getting caught
in a gif's eddy, fanfic of life.
Hit some glistening limit, grope
toward new context, take
with you what you can get.

PREMONITION

☆

It's like this: soft-core
knowledge, symptoms

of certainty fill me
like helium, keep whole

days at a hover. Thrill
chatters through limbs,

like hitting floor when
expecting more stairs,

stable ground a slow
tackle from below. Talk

to me about what lives
inside the body waiting

for the body to come
around. Let's talk rooms

we've known, strewn
with evidence of failed

feng shui. We share this
interest in what might be,

but isn't. We have to.
Heavier elements tug back.

We all know blinking
is sleeping on the job

that is being alive, spread
out over time. No one

cares. Only you blink
like an operator, like this

is your Morse, pinging
facts having a crack

at the droning,
pleasant known.

If you've found a way
to hold two things

in mind at once,
I'd love to know it.

Thing is, I'm reaching
for you all the time.

CROWD SOURCE

☆

Outside, the street.
Houses close their
wooden eyelids,
mumble: *Don't want*
you to see me this way.
Everything is so
crowded with distance.
Vacancy gets right up
in your grill, coming
at you with a group
hug, saying you, too,
can be a part of this.
Just hear me out.

TOO NEGATIVE

☆

I was a kid other kids'
parents gossiped about.

They told their children
what I was: *too negative.*

I get it. Fair to fear
contagion of bad attitudes,

to think naming a thing
can be an inoculation.

Of course my friends
filled me in. Of course

I took my diagnosis
lying down on mostly

frozen sand. Loose
grains made their way

to my scalp. Stayed there
for a few thousand years.

FALSE NEGATIVES

☆

Fact: that which is accidental
is extraneous to survival.

Being ready is a register
of attitude, not behaviour.

Don't look to your hands
for answers – nothing

you need is visible.
It's about the air as a medium,

about what you don't know
you know before you begin.

—

I search for facts about survival,
find *The Top 100 Items to Disappear First.*

—

40. Big Dogs (and plenty of dog food)

32. Garden Seeds (Non-Hybrid)

19. Baby Supplies: Diapers/formula, ointments/aspirin, etc.

—

Here's the scenario where I'm pregnant
by accident. Turn of events in which

I get a thing I want, just not enough
to choose it. Great – no need to give

up my favourite ways to see myself:
long-standing disappearing act,

leave-no-trace camper in my own life.
I'm not saying it's responsible,

only that it's true: I prefer to think
I am a consequence, never an origin.

That's the basic sketch.
Details to be filled in later.

—

Lying in wait for what hasn't happened
but could, items stocked in the basement
find comfort in having been brought there
with purpose. The cans piled in the corner
make a claim for unity, which, of course,
can be measured in degrees. They feel
their parts are more than accidental, held
together by a common cause. This unity ranks
above, say, a party, but below a human being.

—

47. Journals, Diaries & Scrapbooks

94. Wine/Liquors (for bribes, medicinal, etc.)

17. Survival Guidebook

—

Questions we must demand of an event:
Is it happening? And then: *Is it happening now?*

—

Naming a substance is an act of feeling
for principles of unity. Line up every
feature that can be lost before a thing
can no longer be what it is. Every
item you can ditch without collapsing
the whole is considered an accident.

—

5. Lamp Oil, Wicks, Lamps, Lanterns

24. Feminine Hygiene/Haircare/Skin products

7. Guns, Ammunition, Pepper Spray, Knives, Clubs, Bats & Slingshots

67. Board Games, Cards, Dice

———

A tide is all about rising.
Ascent is a motion progress
has claimed for its own.

What if you know the event
is happening, but you don't
know who you're in it with?

———

Lists of possible outcomes are mostly
about endings. This is not a necessity,
only a tendency of the form.

———

The cans' argument is twofold.
One: they are bound by virtue
of being literally piled (i.e., coming
together to form the unity of a pile).
Two: as a list made manifest, they are
held by the invisible formation of shared
purpose. They have been named
as necessities to survive some future
event that cannot yet be defined.
What we know now: neither cause
nor effect. Just scale. Just magnitude.

—

They say keep two of everything.
One to use, one to bargain with.

—

I'm trying to be more honest
about what all this looking ahead

is really for. It's no accident
that I'm getting into it now.

Once you possess a thing, all
that's left to imagine is losing it.

—

Thing is, I want to disappear first.

—

Aware I'm fighting with boxed-up
flaked light tuna no sodium added,
I still say the argument is false.

It doesn't quite square with a logic
I feel more than I know. Something
about requiring external sources

of intention to make a whole.
Something about how I want to kick
over every goddamn pile I ever see.

GOOD COMEBACK

☆

I'm not doing anything new, just pointing to
what you already knew was there. You've
noticed how the same words keep coming up?

It's like that one recurring hair on my chest:
I've set my phone to tell me when to pluck
it out. That the memory of my own intention

could be kept in my pocket by a fragment
of light is one reason I don't wish myself
into the past anymore. Which doesn't mean

I've stopped playing the game of reaching
back, feeling for events with some give,
seeing how much torsion memory can take

before the present reveals itself to be one
line item on an agenda of outcomes up
for discussion. I see how this could become

unsettling, to know yourself as unnecessary.
But new contingencies keep meeting me
where I am, like a treadmill's false asphalt

telling me temporary can feel grounded.
That hair comes through my chest's exact
middle, like it's a message from my core,

which is one part of myself I've put some
work into. One of these days the hair will
open its tiny face and speak: *Save as new.*

INTENT

☆

Glass on glass, shot drops
into pint, and there it is:
atmospheric storm on some

outer planet, or what was
called one, could still be
should we choose to classify

bodies by what we know
about recoil. Some errors
are just a way of being

right. No matter the parts,
we are in a system. I'm
talking to a scholar who says

she studies what it means
to intend to do something.
I know a bit about this, how

the future is a condition
we live with now. Checklist
of symptoms in my wallet:

inability to tunnel vision,
phantom carpal tunnel,
conjectural carpe diem.

I ask whether anything
but a feeling could be more
than a feeling. She says: *No*

regrets for what you haven't seen. Says: Be the ghost you want to see in the machine.

POINT OF CONTACT

☆

The other day, I watched
your eyelid get stuck on itself
long enough to seem like it was
a message about what looking
demands. You laughed, only
it was more like laughing was
a retriever biting you across
the throat, shaking you down
with the certainty of answering
to a code more ancient than
pleasure. You kept your hand
over the eye as you folded
toward the table and I knew,
then, I would give you anything
that promises to grow back.

PREDICTIVE TEXT

☆

Left a note to myself
on the counter. Bald
side up, it drinks all
the light. Fear is, to
turn it over would
foretell my standing
here, not turning
it over. The record
of last night's me
knowing I'd be here,
stuck with one foot
in the nearest verb
tense like a pervert
enjoying a soaker.
What follows from
what you know is
not the same thing
as knowledge. Even
when you get it right.

HONEYMOON

☆

Official advice: do not touch
the water. Here's the berm,

and here's you. That hungry,
broken line of overreach

is a phantom wave. If you
play tag with the ocean,

you will lose. We are
the sort to heed warnings:

from the safety zone we watch
the water stage small

uprisings, heaving gestures
of ocean that eat their own

advance. We kill days keeping
an eye on progress. Then drive,

slalom the highway doodled
in the margin of panoramas

one-upping each other the long
way down the coast. I daydream

your death, see how far
I can tether from the wheel,

letting the absence at the end
of our contract loom. I have

such sick driving skills. This is
commitment. No biggie if you fall

asleep, we'll still find our way
back to the view, front-row seats

furrowed into the shelled-out
length of beach. One night,

we stay so long the light leaves
us alone with the ocean making big

plans it reneges on, taking whole
generations of wannabe sand down

with it. The fog tapers in, and out
of the dark, that fragile upright

shadow, human and wavering,
flowing to the water. *You're it.*

I'M STARING AT MY PHONE

☆

Because I'm looking for emoji
to mean elisions, knots of nothing
in a brain. I know there are two
kinds of lesions – those that occupy
space, and those that don't – and still
I can't name the accumulated not-there
that sucker-punched your fatty sheath
one fall, left its trace in the form of gaps,
ceasing the friendly fire of your nerves
for a time that's since turned apocryphal,
not in the telling, but in the dozy quiet
of not hearing from a thing at all.
You can't call an event original until
it comes back. Tradition is made
through repetition. Through recurrence.
What we learn to live for: nothing
happening. The everyday risk of quiet
and its rupture. I stroke the screen,
consider options, settle: shadow
head, shit stack, crystal ball, bomb.

NOTES

≈

The symbols used as section titles and subtitles – circle, cross, square, star, and waves – are based on Zener cards, which are used to test for extrasensory perception. Invented in the 1930s by psychologist Karl Zener, the cards were used in experiments conducted by Zener and parapsychologist J.B. Rhine. The results of these experiments have since been attributed to "sensory leakage": the transference of the card's images through shadow, reflection, and other conventionally perceptible means.

p. 1. Beetle in a box = Wittgenstein; kitty in a box = Schrödinger.

p. 8. An accident is any feature or property that could be taken away from a thing without changing what that thing is. Essence is anything that can't be taken away. Aristotle said it first. The idea that unity comes in degrees is from Augustine.

p. 12. Cows only have four stomachs.

p. 22. The Knowledge is the navigational test required of cab drivers in London, England. It does not affect the internalization of linguistic forms but can change the brain in other ways.

p. 28. #nofilter is used on Instagram to indicate that a photo is unedited.

p. 30. Yolo = You only live once.

p. 43. Phil is arguably the original Groundhog Day groundhog. He lives in Punxsutawney, Pennsylvania. He is more than 130 years old.

p. 47. E-Prime, or English-Prime, is a version of the English language that excludes all forms of the verb "to be."

p. 59. A list of "The Top 100 Items to Disappear First" can be found on SurvivalCache.com.

p. 68. "The ghost in the machine" is a (derisive) description of Cartesian mind-body dualism coined by philosopher Gilbert Ryle.

ACKNOWLEDGEMENTS

≋

Thank you to the editors of *Maisonneuve*, *Prelude*, *Prism International*, and *The Puritan* for publishing versions of some of these poems.

Thank you to the Toronto Arts Council, the Canada Council for the Arts, The Banff Centre, and The Ohio State University for supporting the completion of this project.

Thank you to Kathy Fagan, Angus Fletcher, Mikko Harvey, Andrew Hudgins, and Maggie Smith.

Thank you to Anita Chong, the McClelland & Stewart poetry board, Andrew Roberts, and other people at M&S I don't know yet whose labour will go into this book.

Thank you to Kevin Connolly, whom I am lucky to count as a mentor and a friend.

Thank you to my family, the circle around which keeps widening.

& Thank you to Andrew, who lets the future in.

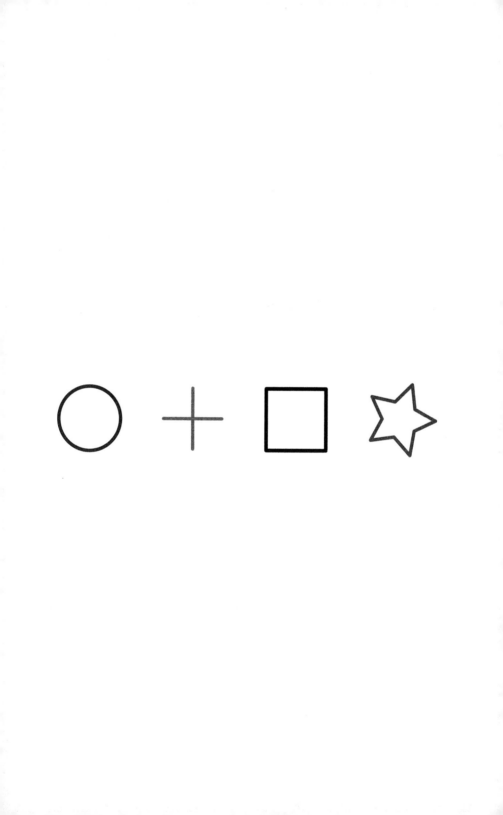